The Book of Norma

Guidance & Prayers
on Living a God-Driven Life

By Norma Jean Moore

Dedicated to Norma's Grandchildren
Pilar, Keir Jr., Malaya, Nahla & Micah

The quotes in this book were transcribed from a prayer journal that Norma Jean Moore kept from October 11, 2013 to August 3, 2014, while reading *Draw the Circle: The 40 Day Prayer Challenge* by Mark Batterson and writing about the many things she desired for her life and her family. In the last season of her life—and perhaps all of her adult life—she had made a practice of writing to and about God in journals.

In reading her writings, it is clear that one of her foremost and constant prayers was to be a vehicle to share what she had learned through studying His teachings and striving to live a God-driven life. This book represents what I hope is an answer to this simple yet bold prayer that can be used to encourage and inspire family and friends.

With Love,

Chaz Kyser
Norma's daughter-in-law

The best answer is always
what brings God the most glory.

We are not to despise small beginnings,
for the Lord rejoices when we take steps
in the right direction. We do the little
things; God does the big things.

Have vision beyond your resources! Don't
limit God but be responsible. God owns
the cattle on a thousand hills, but we
forget and butcher our dreams.

There are times when we must be willing to give up something we have or desire to God in order to get it back from God! It will probably be something precious to us. God will test us to make sure the gift is not more important than Him, or the dream more important than Him, or that it is not an idol to us. If so, the dream, gift, person, ect., may need to die in our desires so it can be resurrected by God. When he gives it back, we realize it has to be handled as something to be stewarded so He gets the glory.

God is never late. He is always on time.
He prepares good works in advance.
We are not to lose faith or lose heart or
lose hope. We must keep asking,
keep seeking, keep knocking!

God is NOT offended by our prayers for
the impossible. God is not pleased when
we ask him to do things we can do for
ourselves. Impossible prayers honor
God and they reveal our faith and
allow God to reveal His glory.

We take on more responsibilities, debt, etc., than we can handle and then get sick, depressed, unhappy, distraught, and worried because we don't know how to handle all we've taken on. Simplify your life, let go of all your worries, and let Father God deal with you and the issues and responsibilities you have assumed!

Faith is a verb, not a noun.

Remember, God can do it.

He is bigger than our dreams,

our problems, and our mistakes.

Since my God knows no limits,

neither will my prayers.

God is honored when we act as if He is
going to answer our prayers. After you
pray, you need to take a small step of
faith, which often turns into giant leaps.

Stepping out on faith,
the first step is usually the hardest,
longest, most awkward. After the first
step, we will see signs followed
by an avalanche of blessings.

Pray and stay (in Faith). In other words,
pray and believe God will give you what
you are believing for. You won't have to
work, borrow, or figure out a way to get
it. That's God's department and job.
Yours is to pray, believe, and have faith in
God; He will do the rest. Stay out of it,
because if God gave you the desire, it's
His job to fulfil it, not yours. He has so
much in store for you if you just let Him
do what He does best—be God.

If we would all begin to pray for others, not so much for ourselves, we would see major changes in the world.

Instead of meditating (talking and thinking) about what you want or don't have, or what you would like or don't currently like, focus on meditating on the Word of God. Be consistent in this.

Listen for God's voice;
He's waiting to talk to you and with you.
Stay away from sin.
Get serious with God.

I believe God causes us to wait
for the answers to prayers to build
our faith muscles so they can get
stronger by the day, because we will
continuously need strong, hard faith for
the bigger blessings to come.

God knows I can't be stopped, nor will I
stop doing His will. He has a plan for me
and I am determined to follow it.

Prayers are eternal. Our prayers are not limited because God is not limited. When we pray to God who dwells outside our space/time continuum (where we live), He takes the prayer, works it, and when He answers it, He reopens the door from his limitless eternity into our space/time continuum and lets the answer come back in. Hallelujah! His answer is right outside and you never know when He's going to open the door with the answer.

God births a desire in our heart and then waters it with love, as we pray about it and bathe it in prayer. Lord help me to dream big with your dreams and be smack dab in the middle of your will for me.

I will keep seeking, asking, knocking until all God has shown me and put in my heart has come to pass in His own timing.

Sometimes God is saying to us, "Wait for it. Wait for it," so He sometimes says "No, not now," or "No, not yet." I have several no, not now's and no, not yet's . . . but I believe He will open doors, open windows, and pour out blessings too numerous for me to keep to myself and I will be able to share them with others anytime, anywhere, anyhow.

Lord, please help me to live an extraordinary life filled with extraordinary (crazy) prayers asked and answered by you! Please give me extraordinary desires—God given—to ask you so you can answer them.
Lord, I am open to hear,
receive, and do Your will.

God has a plan, an agenda, for me and my family. Bless the Lord. I receive it!

The more we give to God, the more we have and the more we become.

Whatever my Father God desires for me, I accept. He had great desires for me.
He has thoughts about me.
He wants to prosper me!

God sometimes calls us to ante up our faith and then let the chips fall where they may. I like this because it's exciting and fun to see how He will work out the details.

God honors
those who pray with audacity.
Pray on it and then act on it.

We are not patient with God or our
prayers. We want to reap the very second
we sow. We want microwave answers; we
want our answers immediately. God is
NOT like that. We must have patience; we
must have foresight; we must have the
mindset of a sower. We can't make things
grow—we are the planters of seed (prayers);
God grows (brings) the increase.

I must not let fear dictate my dreams
or decisions. Let my vision determine
the budget; not the budget
determine the vision.

Please help me Lord to see and seize the
opportunities that are all around me all the
time. Please open my eyes and heart.

Faith keeps dreams alive
and they germinate beneath
the surface just like seeds.

What gets celebrated, gets replicated.
Testimonies double as prophecies.

The Lord establishes our steps

The Lord determines our steps

The Lord prepares our steps

The Lord sets in place our steps

The Lord directs our steps

The Lord firmly decides our steps

The Lord makes secure our steps

Praise the Lord

We are impatient with God and our
prayers. We want to reap the moment we
sow. But seeds need time to germinate,
grow, surface. We can't *make* things grow.
We can plant, water, wait.
God gives the increase when He's ready for
us to receive the increase!

Prayers go unanswered because
they are not asked. We never know when
or how God will answer our prayers.
God works in mysterious, wonderful ways.
Don't try to put Him in
a box or try to figure Him out.

If my cause, my desire,

my dream is ordained by God,

any battle I have belongs to God.

It's His victory too, not mine.

When we give our lives to the Lord, we
never know who we will meet, where we
will be led, or what we will be given to do.

This time Lord, I just want to follow Your
lead, go where you are leading me with
YOUR will. Not trying to figure out or plan
what I want or think I need to do.

Ask God to give you vision beyond your resources. God stretches our faith so we will dream bigger dreams.

God is honored when we act as if He is going to answer our prayers. Take small steps of faith after you pray to Him. The small steps of faith turn into giant leaps.

I have crazy faith. God honors those who defy protocol with their bold prayers. God honors those who pray with audacity.

How excellent is my Lord who
orchestrates my life each day and brings
together everything to encourage
me to greater accomplishments.

Prayer is an investment
that accumulates compound interest.

Some things can only be conceived,
imagined, revealed by the Holy Spirit. We
have to cultivate the Holy Spirit. He helps
us see the invisible and hear the inaudible.

Practice good financial management.

Count the cost of each vision.

Be a good steward of God's money and
resources He blesses you to handle.

God listens more to our heart than to our
words. He is looking for child-like faith.

Faith is not faith until it is acted upon.

You are never really prepared for
what God puts in your heart to do.

As we press into God's presence,
old sinful desires die, new holy desires
are birthed in our spirit, and these
desires become lifelong dreams if we
nurture these desires in prayer.

Trust that God knows exactly what you
need and turn each need into a prayer.
Record each need and each prayer
and each answer to the prayer.

Waiting does not delay God's plans
and purpose; it expedites them.
Waiting is the fast track to whatever it is
God wants us to do in our lives.

Let the Holy Spirit come upon you
and help you to think new thoughts
and feel new feelings. Wait for God.

God speaks to you through his Word, then
He speaks thru you to others.

Don't have unconfessed sin in your life.
Get rid of it. It's harmful to you and your
relationship with your heavenly Father.

Sin makes it hard to hear His voice.

Incline your ear to Him and He,

God your Father, will incline His ear

to you. Get close to Him and

you won't miss anything He says.

God will call us to do something and

provide whatever we need to accomplish it.

He's that good! He wants us to be

successful in everything we do.

Don't give yourself away to just anyone.

Let God your father be proud as

He gives you to His choice for you.

Please God, give me favor, discernment,
and grace when I meet with others.

God is honored not by prayers that are
within the realm of human possibility,
but by the petition to do what is
humanly impossible or
definitely beyond our capability.

Continue to abide in the Word of God
and it will continue to abide in you.
Linger in God's presence; it causes
Him to linger in you. It allows you to know
exactly what to do each step of the way;
He will reveal mysteries to you.

Prayer makes the forces of darkness retreat.
Our most effective weapon: God's Word.

Stay in the Word of God until you are
motivated by God into action
and not motivated by fear.

When God answers prayers, regardless
of whether they are big or small,
we must share it with others.
We must turn answered prayers
into praise, not into pride.

Norma Jean Moore

March 31, 1945–May 2, 2017

Norma Jean Moore journeyed to be with the Lord on May 2, 2017, after complications from amyloidosis, a rare health condition. She had recently celebrated her 72nd birthday surrounded by family and friends and knew that she was cherished and loved.

The daughter of Herbert and LaVada Newton, Norma was born and raised in San Diego, California, along with her brother, Kenneth. She lived and worked in California to middle adulthood, and earned a bachelor's degree in aviation management from National University.

In 1985, she moved to the East Coast and soon made a home for herself in Virginia. Once there, she built a successful career as a security specialist for government contractors SAIC and then Leidos, where she was well-regarded by her colleagues and managers.

Norma was a vibrant, joyful, and adventurous woman, who lived by the old adage "age ain't nothing but a number." She loved to travel and had the opportunity to visit Zimbabwe, the UK, and China, which she went on during a trip by herself in 2015. Alongside her mother, sons, and friends, she touched the earth of several other countries during cruises, including Barbados, Venezuela, Jamaica, Haiti, the Dominican Republic, and the Bahamas. She also took girls' trips in the United States with her dear friends Doris Noyes and Mary Braswell.

Much of Norma's life centered upon enriching her mind and spirit. From her extensive library in her beautiful home in Woodbridge, Virginia, it is evident that she was a voracious reader, and she had books in all genres. She also attended classes in theology, financial empowerment, and health and wellness—even traveling as far as New York to learn about natural medicine while working full time.

Norma's list of goals was as long in her 70s as it was in her 30s. She had plans to start another career after retirement focused on women's wellness; learn more about Oriental medicine; further study the Word of God so she could minister to others; move to Hawaii, a place she loved for its beauty and tranquility; and buy a huge house with an unobstructed view of the water.

But perhaps what is most notable about Norma is that she was a woman of true faith. She accepted Jesus as her Lord and Savior at a young age at Logan Temple A.M.E Zion Church in San Diego, California. She had many church homes in her life and was proud to last attend First Mount Zion Baptist Church in Dumfries, Virginia. She used the Word of God to uplift others, and was known to friends as a prayer warrior because she constantly spoke affirmations of health, peace, and prosperity over everyone she held dear.

Norma is survived by her brother, Kenneth Newton; sons James and Keir; daughters-in law Pilar and Chaz; and grandchildren Pilar, Keir Jr., Malaya, Nahla, and Micah.

Made in the USA
Las Vegas, NV
11 January 2021

15671236R00020